NATIONAL GEOGRAPHIC LEARNING | CENGAGE Learning

STARTER

W0018747

TIME ZONES

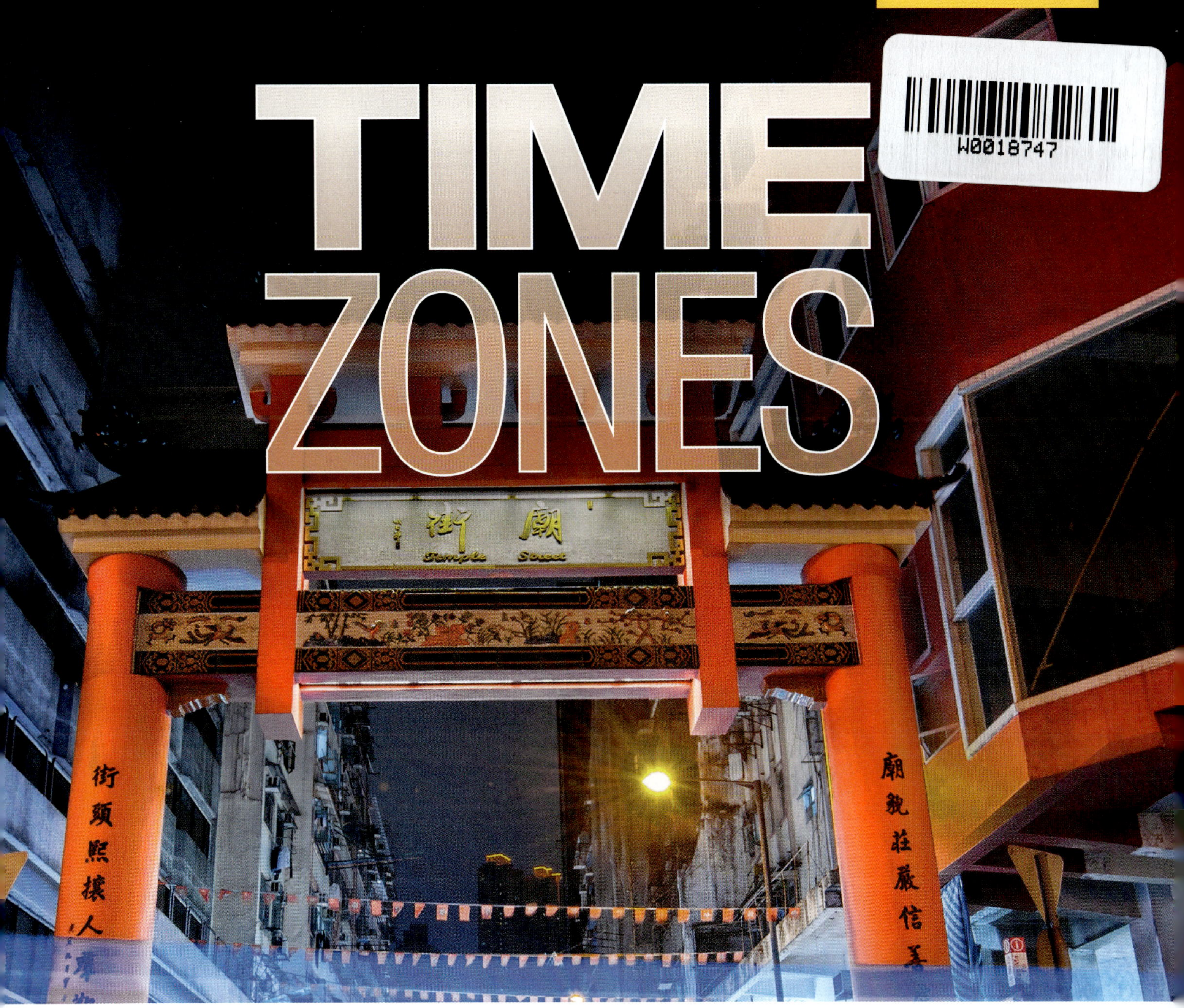

Nicholas Beare

SECOND EDITION

Australia • Brazil • Japan • Korea • Mexico • Singapore • Spain • United Kingdom • United States

Time Zones Starter Combo
Second Edition

Nicholas Beare

Publisher: Andrew Robinson

Senior Development Editor: Derek Mackrell

Development Editors: Charlotte Sharman,
Christopher Street

Assistant Editor: Melissa Pang

Director of Global Marketing: Ian Martin

Product Marketing Manager: Anders Bylund

Media Researcher: Leila Hishmeh

Senior Director of Production:
Michael Burggren

Senior Content Project Manager: Tan Jin Hock

Manufacturing Planner: Mary Beth Hennebury

Compositor: Page 2, LLC.

Cover/Text Design: Creative Director:
Christopher Roy, Art Director: Scott Baker,
Senior Designer: Michael Rosenquest

Cover Photo: ones qiu/500px Prime

ISBN-13: 978-1-305-26031-3

National Geographic Learning
20 Channel Center Street
Boston, MA 02210
USA

Cengage Learning is a leading provider of customized learning solutions with employees residing in nearly 40 different countries and sales in more than 125 countries around the world. Find your local representative at:
international.cengage.com/region

Cengage Learning products are represented in Canada by Nelson Education, Ltd.

Visit National Geographic Learning online at **NGL.Cengage.com**

Visit our corporate website at **www.cengage.com**

Printed in the United States of America
Print Number: 02   Print Year: 2016

Contents

SCOPE AND SEQUENCE

Unit Title	Functions	Grammar	Vocabulary	The Real World	Video
Page 8 **1** **Hello!**	Greetings Describing color	**Greetings:** *Hello. My name's Stig.* *I'm Ming.* *Bye, Maya.* **Demonstratives:** *What's this? It's a computer.* *What's that? It's an eraser.*	The alphabet Classroom items Numbers Colors Days of the week	Colorful Thailand	At the Zoo
Page 20 **2** **Where Is He From?**	Asking and describing where people come from Asking about ages	*Where's Maya from?* *She's from Brazil.* *Where's that?* *It's in South America.* *How old is he?* *He's fifty-five.*	Countries and continents Numbers: 11–100 Ordinal numbers: 1st–10th Months of the year	Seasons	Around the World
Page 32 **3** **This Is My House.**	Asking about day and dates Talking about possessions Asking and describing location of people and things	*What date is it?* *It's September 16th.* *When is your birthday?* **Regular plural nouns:** *dogs, rabbits* **Demonstratives:** *This, that, these, those* **Possessive 's:** *What is the woman's name?* *Where's Robert's pet?*	Ordinal numbers: 11th–31st Special days/celebrations Pets Parts of the body Places around the house	What Do You See?	Otters in the House

Acknowledgements

The author and publisher would like to thank the following individuals and organizations who offered many helpful insights, ideas, and suggestions during the development of **Time Zones**.

Asia and Europe

Phil Woodall, Aoyama Gakuin Senior High School; **Suzette Buxmann**, Aston A+; **Wayne Fong**, Aston English; Berlitz China; Berlitz Germany; Berlitz Hong Kong; Berlitz Japan; Berlitz Singapore; **Anothai Jetsadu**, Cha-am Khunying Nuangburi School; **Rui-Hua Hsu**, Chi Yong High School; Gary Darnell, DEU Private School, Izmir; **Hwang Soon Hee**, **Irean Yeon**, **Junhee Im**, **Seungeun Jung**, Eun Seok Elementary School; **Hyun Ah Park**, Gachon University; **Hsi-Tzu Hung**, Hwa Hsia Institute of Technology; **Kate Sato**, Kitopia English School; **Daniel Stewart**, Kaisei Junior and Senior High School; **Haruko Morimoto**, **Ken Ip**, Mejiro Kenshin Junior and Senior High School; **Sovoan Sem**, Milky Way School; **Shu-Yi Chang**, Ming Dao High School; **Ludwig Tan**, National Institute of Education; **Tao Rui**, **Yuan Wei Hua**, New Oriental Education & Technology Group; **Tom Fast**, Okayama Gakugeikan High School; **Yu-Ping Luo**, Oriental Institute of Technology; **Jutamas**, Prakhanong Pittayalai School; **Akira Yasuhara**, Rikkyo Ikebukuro Junior and Senior High School; **Matthew Rhoda**, Sakuragaoka Junior and Senior High School; **Michael Raship**, **Nicholas Canales**, Scientific Education Group Co; **Andrew O'Brien**, Second Kyoritsu Girls Junior and Senior High School; **Atsuko Okada**, Shinagawa Joshi Gakuin Junior and Senior High School; **Sheila Yu**, Shin Min High School; **Stewart Dorward**, Shumei Junior and Senior High School; **Gaenor Hardy**, Star English Centres; **Philip Chandler**, **Thomas Campagna**, Tama University Meguro Junior and Senior High School; **Lois Wang**, Teachall English; **Iwao Arai**, **James Daly**, **Satomi Kishi**, Tokyo City University Junior and Senior High School; **Jason May**, Tokyo Seitoku University High School; **Amnoui Jaimipak**, Triamudomsuksapattanakarn Chiangrai School; **Jonee de Leon**, Universal English Center; **Thiwaphorn Tharawatcharasart**, Uthaiwitthayakhom School; **Richard Ascough**, Wayo Women's University; **Kirvin Andrew Dyer**, Yan Ping High School.

The Americas

Allynne Fraemam, **Flávia Carneiro**, **Jonathan Reinaux**, **Mônica Carvalho**, ABA; **Antonio Fernando Pinho**, Academia De Idiomas; **Wilmer Escobar**, Academia Militar; **Adriana Rupp**, **Denise Silva**, **Jorge Mendes**, ACBEU; **Rebecca Gonzalez**, AIF Systems English Language Institute; **Camila Vidal Suárez**, **Adriana Yaffe**, **Andrea da Silva**, **Bruno Oliveri**, **Diego A. Fábregas Acosta**, **Fabiana Hernandez**, **Florencia Barrios**, **Ignacio Silveira Trabal**, **Lucía Greco Castro**, **Lucy Pintos**, **Silvia Laborde**, Alianza Cultural Uruguay Estados Unidos; **Adriana Alvarez**, ASICANA; **Corina C. Machado Correa**, **Silvia Helena R. D. Corrêa**, **Mariana M. Paglione Vedana**, Associacao Alumni; Berlitz, Colombia; Berlitz Mexico; Berlitz Peru; Berlitz US; **Simone Ashton**, Britanic Madalena; **Keith Astle**, Britanic Piedade; **Dulce Capiberibe**, Britanic Setúbal; **Matthew Gerard O'Conner**, Britanic Setúbal; **Viviane Remígio**, Britanic Setúbal; **Adriana da Silva**, **Ana Raquel F. F. Campos**, **Ebenezer Macario**, **Giselle Schimaichel**, **Larissa Platinetti**, **Miriam Alves Carnieletto**, **Selma Oliveira**, Centro Cultural Brasil Estados Unidos CCBEU; Amiris Helena, CCDA; Alexandra Nancy Lake Sawada, **Ana Tereza R. P. Moreira**, **Denise Helena Monteiro**, **Larissa Ferreria**, **Patricia Mckay Aronis**, CELLEP; **Claudia Patricia Gutierrez**, **Edna Zapata**, **Leslie Cortés**, **Silvia Elena Martinez**, **Yesid Londoño**, Centro Colombo Americano-Medellin; **Gabriel Villamar Then**, Centro Educativo los Prados; **Monica Lugo**, Centro Escolar Versalles; **Adriane Caldas**, **Simone Raupp**, **Sylvia Formoso**, Colégio Anchieta; **José Olavo de Amorim**, Colégio Bandeirantes; **Dionisio Alfredo Meza Solar**, Colegio Cultural I; **Madson Gois Diniz**, Colegio De Aplicação; **Ilonka Diaz**, **Melenie Gonzalez**, Colegio Dominico Espanol; **Laura Monica Cadena**, **Rebeca Perez**, Colegio Franco Ingles; **Jedinson Trujillo**, Colegio Guías; **Christophe Flaz**, **Isauro Sanchez Gutierrez**, Colegio Iglesa Bautista Fundamenta; **Ayrton Lambert**, Colégio II Peretz; **Samuel Jean Baptiste**, Colegio Instituto Montessori; **Beatriz Galvez**, **Evelyn Melendez**, Colegio Los Olivos; **Carlos Gomez**, **Diana Herrera Ramirez**, **Diana Pedraza Aguirre**, **Karol Bibana Hutado Morales**, Colegio Santa Luisa; **Marta Segui Rivas**, Colegio Velmont; **Thays Ladosky**, DAMAS; **Amalia Vasquez**, **Ana Palencia**, **Fernando de Leon**, **Isabel Cubilla**, **Leonel Zapata**, **Lorena Chavarria**, **Maria Adames**, English Access Microscholarship Program; **Rosângela Duarte Dos Santos**, English Space; **Walter Junior Ribeiro Silva**, Friends Language Center; **Luis Reynaldo Frias**, Harvard Institute; **Carlos Olavo Queiroz Guimarães**, **Elisa Borges**, **Patricia Martins**, **Lilian Bluvol Vaisman**, **Samara Camilo Tomé Costa**, IBEU; **Gustavo Sardo**, **João Carlos Queiroz Furtado**, **Rafael Bastos**, **Vanessa Rangel**, IBLE; **Graciela Martin**, ICANA (BELGRANO); **Carlos Santanna**, **Elizabeth Gonçalves**, ICBEU; **Inês Greve Milke**, **João Alfredo Bergmann**, Instituto Cultural Brasileiro Norte-Americano; **Tarsis Perez**, ICDA-Instituto Cultural Dominico Americano; **Cynthia Marquez**, **Guillermo Cortez**, **Ivan Quinteros**, **Luis Morales R**, **Melissa Lopez**, **Patricia Perez**, **Rebeca de Arrue**, **Rebeca Martinez de Arrue**, Instituto Guatemalteco Americano; **Renata Lucia Cardoso**, Instituto Natural de Desenvolvimento Infantil; **Graciela Nobile**, Instituto San Diego; **Walter Guevara**, Pio XII; **Juan Omar Valdez**, Professional Training Systems; **Carlos Carmona**, **Eugenio Altieri**, **Regan Albertson**, Progressive English Services; **Raul Billini**, Prolingua; **Juan Manuel Marin**, **Luisa Fecuanda Infort**, **Maria Consuelo Araujo**, Providencia; **Carmen Gehrke**, Quatrum, Porto Alegre; **Rodrigo Rezende**, Seven; **Lcuciano Joel del Rosario**, St. José School; **Sabino Morla**, UASD; Silvia Regina D'Andrea, União Cultural Brasil-Estados Unidos; **Ruth Salomon-Barkemeyer**, Unilínguas Sao Leopoldo; **Anatalia Souza**, **Livia Rebelo**, UNIME-Ingles Para Criancas-Salvador; **Andrei dos Santos Cunha**, **Brigitte Mund**, **Gislaine Deckmann**, **Jeane Blume Cortezia**, **Rosana Gusmão**, Unisinos; **Diego Pérez**, Universidad de Ibague; **Beatriz Daldosso Felippe**, U.S. Idiomas Universe School

The author would like to thank the editorial team for their valuable suggestions and advice.

Meet the **Time Zones Team.**

Maya **Ming** **Nadine** **Stig**

This is
Maya Santos,
from Rio de Janeiro,
in Brazil. She's into
music, singing, and
shopping.

This is
Ming Chen,
from Shanghai,
in China. He likes
sports and animals.

This is
Nadine Barnard,
from Cape Town, in South
Africa. She loves nature,
movies, and music.

This is
Stig Andersson,
from Stockholm, in
Sweden. He loves food,
photography, and sports.

1

HELLO!

Preview

Talk with a partner.

1. How do you say hello in your country?

2. How do people in other countries say hello?

Students in the U.S. say hello.

Greetings

A 🎧 01 **Listen and read.**

CONTRACTIONS

My name's	=	My name is
I'm	=	I am

1. Hello. My name's Stig.
   Hi. I'm Nadine.

2. Bye, Maya.
   Bye, Ming.

B 🎧 02 **Listen.** Write a–d in the order you hear the people.

1. 2. *a* 3. 4.

C **Talk with a partner.** Say hello and goodbye.

Hi. My name's Lucy.

Hello, Lucy. I'm Fred.

Bye, Fred!

Bye, Lucy!

Students say hello in New Zealand.

The Alphabet

A 🎧 03 **Listen and repeat.**

Aa	Bb	Cc	Dd	Ee	Ff	Gg
Hh	Ii	Jj	Kk	Ll	Mm	Nn
Oo	Pp	Qq	Rr	Ss	Tt	Uu
Vv	Ww	Xx	Yy	Zz		

CAPITAL LETTERS

Capital letters — **S**tig / **M**aya / **N**adine

B 🎧 04 **Listen.** Write a–e in the order you hear the words.

hello _____   hi _____   name _a_   bye _____   my _____

C **Work with a partner.** Write a list of the people in your class.

What's your name?

My name's Sam.

How do you spell that?

S-A-M.

Sophia

Eric

Tomas

Anita

Unit 1   **11**

In the Classroom

A 🎧 05 **Listen.** Label the photo.

pen	eraser
chair	pencil
paper	~~board~~
book	desk
computer	dictionary

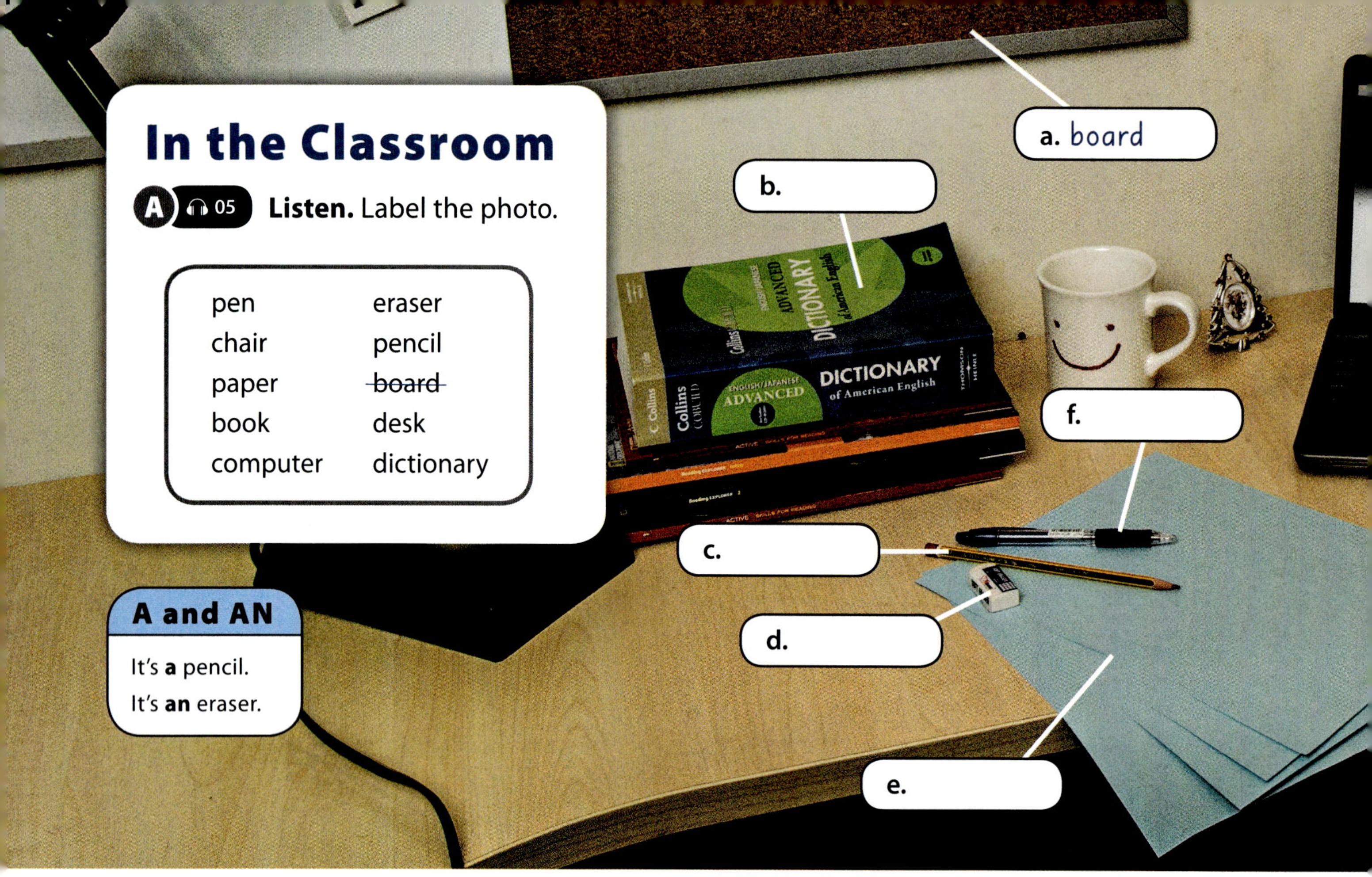

a. board

b.

c.

d.

e.

f.

B 🎧 06 **Listen and read.** Repeat the conversation. Replace the words in **blue**.

1
What's this?
It's **a computer**.

a chair
a dictionary

2
What's that?
It's **an eraser**.

a pencil
a book

C **Talk with a partner.** Use *this* and *that* to talk about things in your classroom.

What's this?

It's a chair.

How do you spell that?

C–H–A–I–R.

g.

h.

i.

j.

Numbers

A 🎧 07 **Listen and repeat.**

◯	1	2	3	4	5	6	7	8	9	10
zero	one	two	three	four	five	six	seven	eight	nine	ten

B 🎧 08 **Listen.** Circle the correct number.

a. 1 ③ 5   b. 2 0 1   c. 7 5 6   d. 4 9 8

e. 3 1 7   f. 8 6 2   g. 10 7 0   h. 2 3 10

i. 9 5 2   j. 4 6 8   k. 3 9 0

C **Talk with a partner.** Say your telephone number.

641-0120

Colors

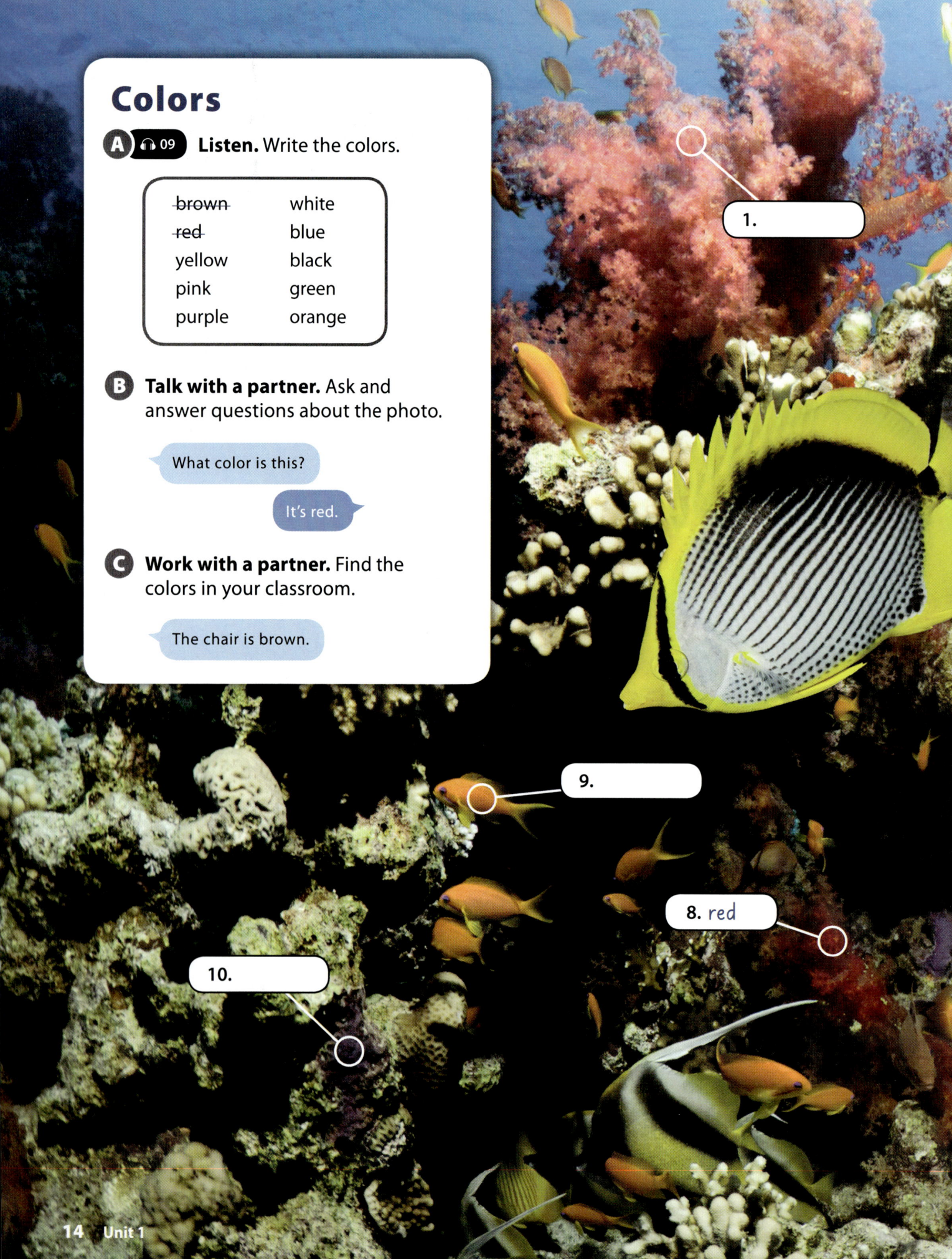

A 🎧 09 **Listen.** Write the colors.

~~brown~~	white
~~red~~	blue
yellow	black
pink	green
purple	orange

B **Talk with a partner.** Ask and answer questions about the photo.

What color is this?

It's red.

C **Work with a partner.** Find the colors in your classroom.

The chair is brown.

1.

9.

8. red

10.

2.

3.

4.

5.

6.

7. brown

Days of the Week

November

Monday	Tuesday	Wednesday	Thursday	Friday	Saturday	Sunday
1	2	3	4	5	6	7
8	9	10	11	12	13	14
15	16	17	18	19	20	21
22	23	24	25	26	27	28
29	30					

2021

A 🎧 10 **Listen.** Complete the words.

1. M <u>o</u> <u>n</u> d a y

2. T u __ __ d __ y

3. __ e d __ __ s d __ __

4. T h u __ __ __ __ y

5. __ r __ d __ y

6. __ __ __ u r d a __

7. S __ n __ a y

B **Talk with a partner.** Ask and answer questions about the days of the week.

What day is it today?

It's Tuesday.

What day is tomorrow?

It's Wednesday.

And yesterday?

Colorful Thailand

In Thailand, there is a color for every day of the week. There are umbrellas for every day!

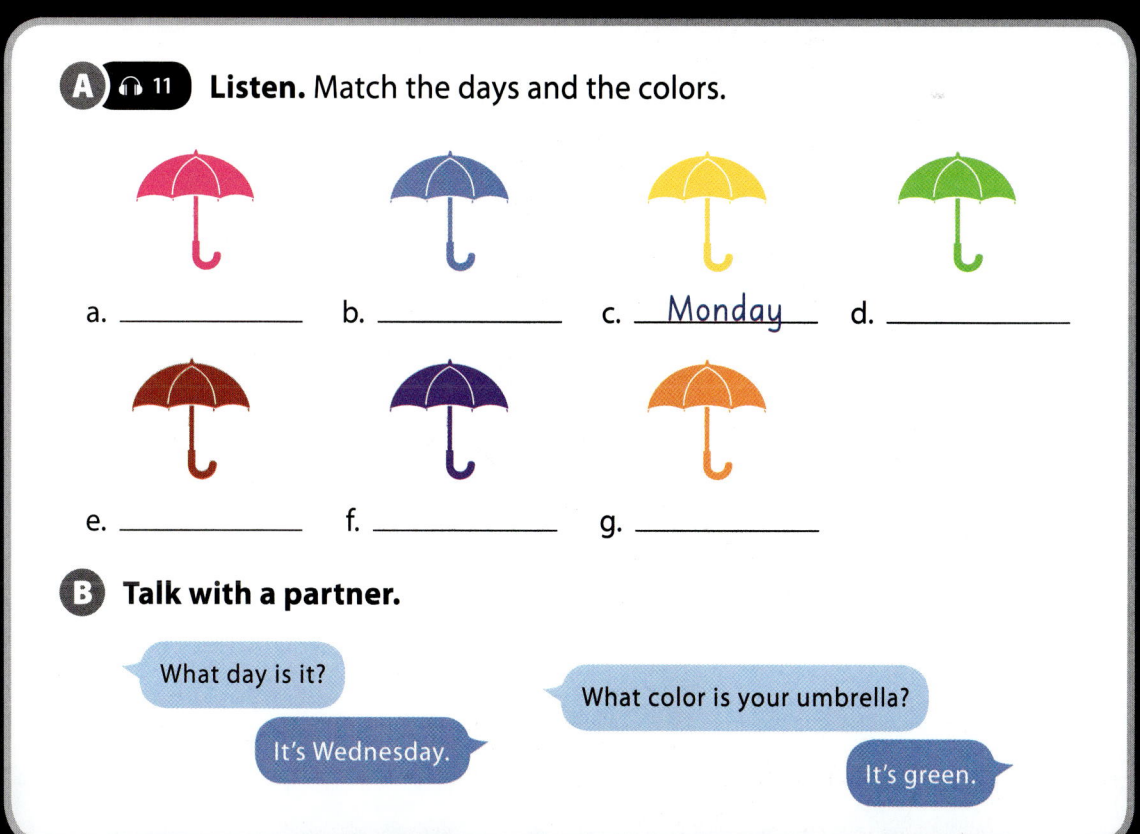

A 🎧 11 **Listen.** Match the days and the colors.

a. _____

b. _____

c. <u>Monday</u>

d. _____

e. _____

f. _____

g. _____

B Talk with a partner.

What day is it?

What color is your umbrella?

It's Wednesday.

It's green.

At the Zoo

ABOUT THE VIDEO

This is a red panda. His name is Farley.

A red panda

BEFORE YOU WATCH

Circle the correct answers. What colors are on the panda?

white   green   (brown)   red   black   blue

WHILE YOU WATCH

Watch the video. Put the sentences in order.

_____ How do you spell that?

_____ F-A-R-L-E-Y.

__1__ What's that?

_____ It's a red panda.

_____ What color is he?

__4__ His name's Farley.

_____ Cool! What's his name?

_____ He's red, white, brown, and black.

AFTER YOU WATCH

Talk with a partner. Practice the conversation in the video.

What's that?

It's a red panda.

WHERE IS HE
FROM?

The 2014 Winter
Olympics in Russia

the United Kingdom

Macedonia

Brazil

Preview

Talk with a partner. Ask and answer questions about the people in the photo.

What country is he from?

He's from South Korea.

Portugal

South Korea

Romania

France

Countries and Continents

A 🎧 12 **Listen.** Number the continents on the map.

> 1. ~~Asia~~ 2. Europe 3. Australia 4. North America
> 5. Africa 6. Antarctica 7. South America

B 🎧 13 **Listen.** Complete the information about each person.

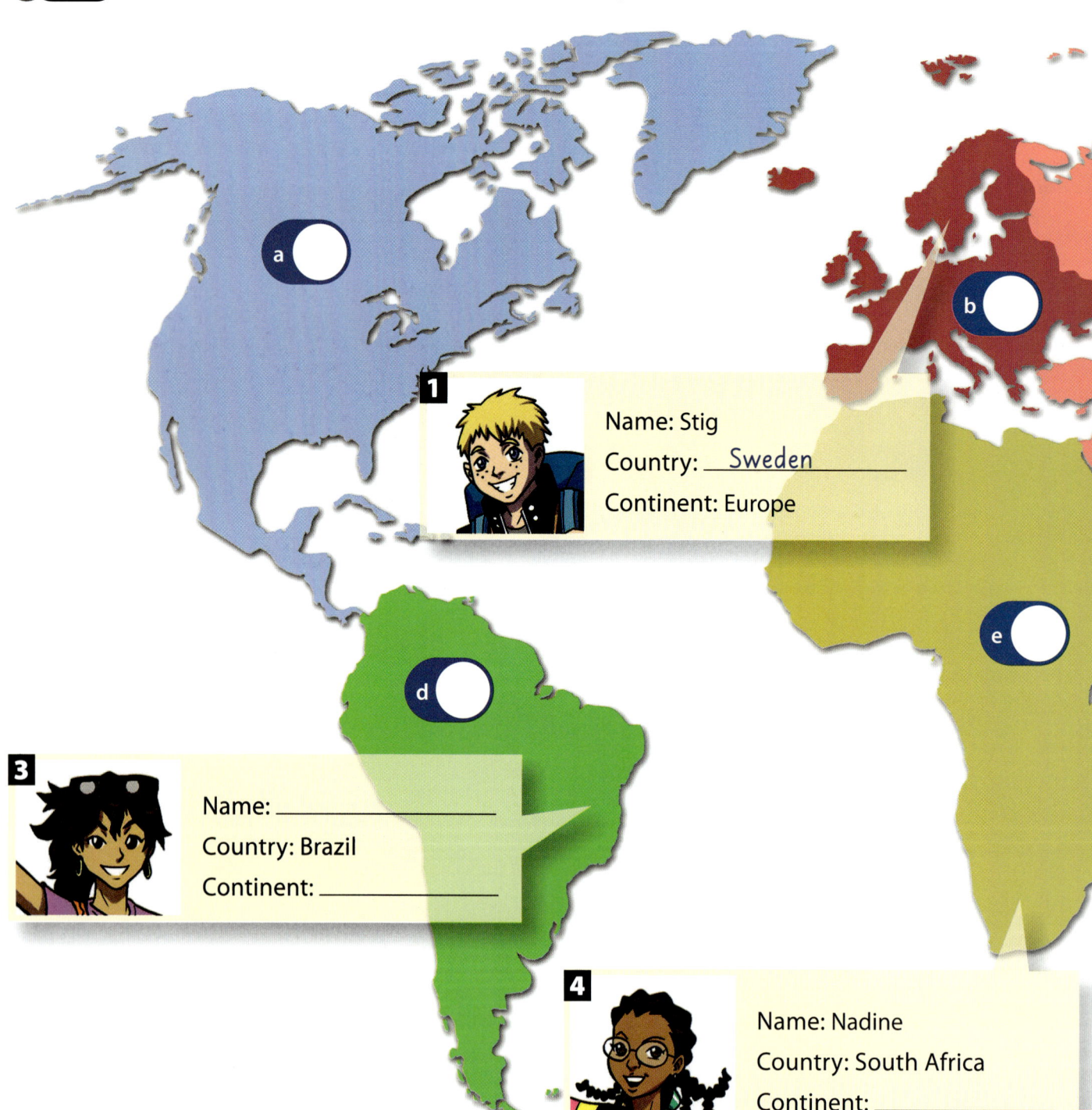

1
Name: Stig
Country: _Sweden_
Continent: Europe

3
Name: _____
Country: Brazil
Continent: _____

4
Name: Nadine
Country: South Africa
Continent: _____

C Work with a partner. Talk about countries and continents.

Sweden is in Europe.

How do you spell Sweden?

S-W-E-D-E-N.

D Complete the chart.

Name	1. _____	2. _____
Alex	Brazil	South America
Elsa	China	Asia
Michael	Canada	North America
Sofia	Spain	Europe
Claire	South Africa	Africa

E Work with a partner. Talk about the people from the chart.

Where's Alex from?

He's from Brazil.

Where's that?

It's in South America.

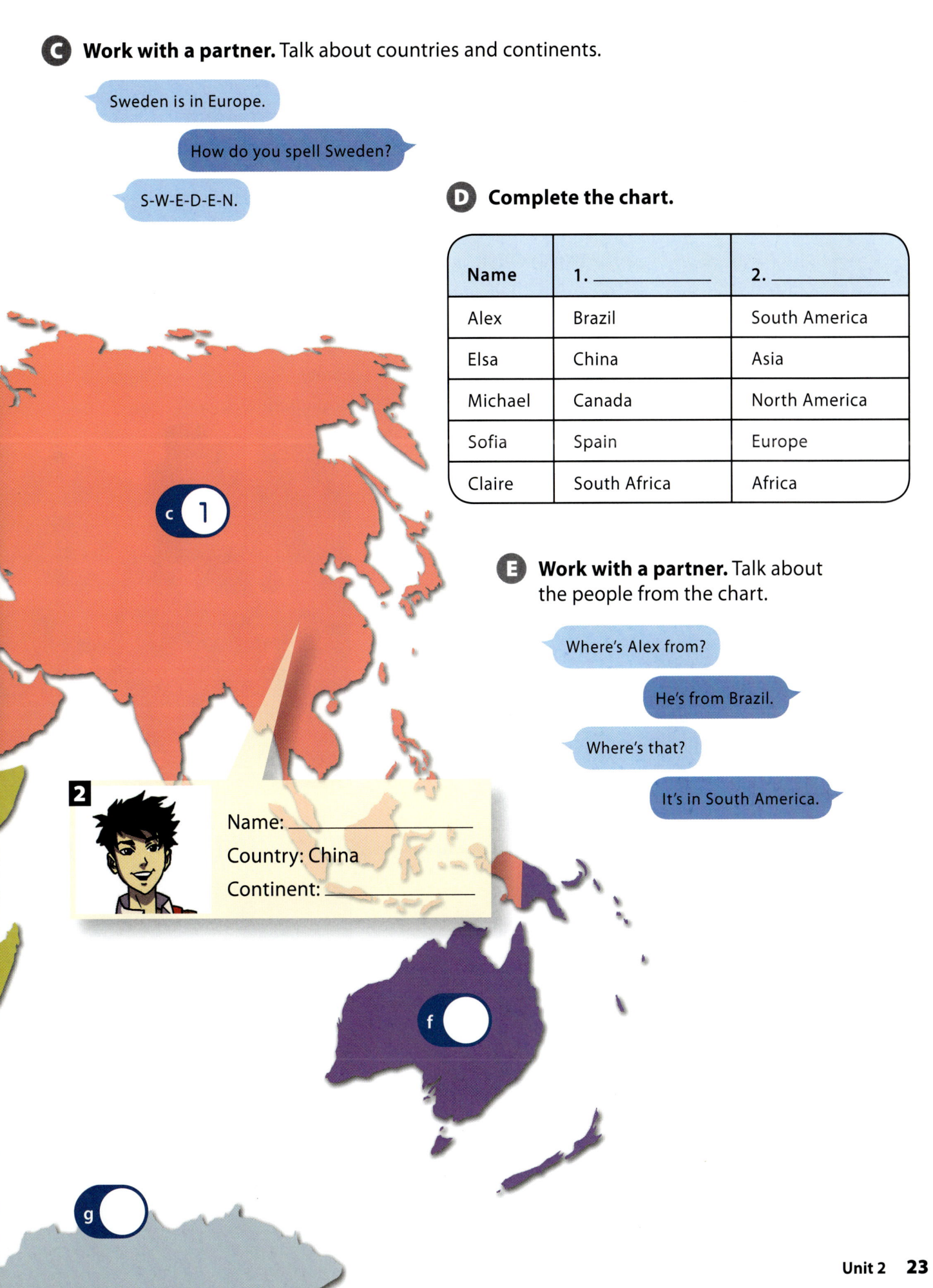

Name: _____
Country: China
Continent: _____

Numbers 11 to 100

A 🎧 14 **Listen and repeat.**

11	eleven	20	twenty	29	twenty-nine
12	twelve	21	twenty-one	30	thirty
13	thirteen	22	twenty-two	40	forty
14	fourteen	23	twenty-three	50	fifty
15	fifteen	24	twenty-four	60	sixty
16	sixteen	25	twenty-five	70	seventy
17	seventeen	26	twenty-six	80	eighty
18	eighteen	27	twenty-seven	90	ninety
19	nineteen	28	twenty-eight	100	a hundred

B 🎧 15 **Listen.** Write the numbers you hear.

a. _____twelve_____   e. _____

b. _____   f. _____

c. _____   g. _____

d. _____   h. _____

C **Play a game. Student A:** Think of a number between ten and a hundred. **Student B:** Guess Student A's number.

Twenty.

Thirty.

Higher.

Lower.

D 🎧 16 **Listen.** Complete the labels about the people in the photo.

E **Work with a partner.** Talk about the people.

What's his name?

His name's Amin.

How old is he?

He's fifty-five.

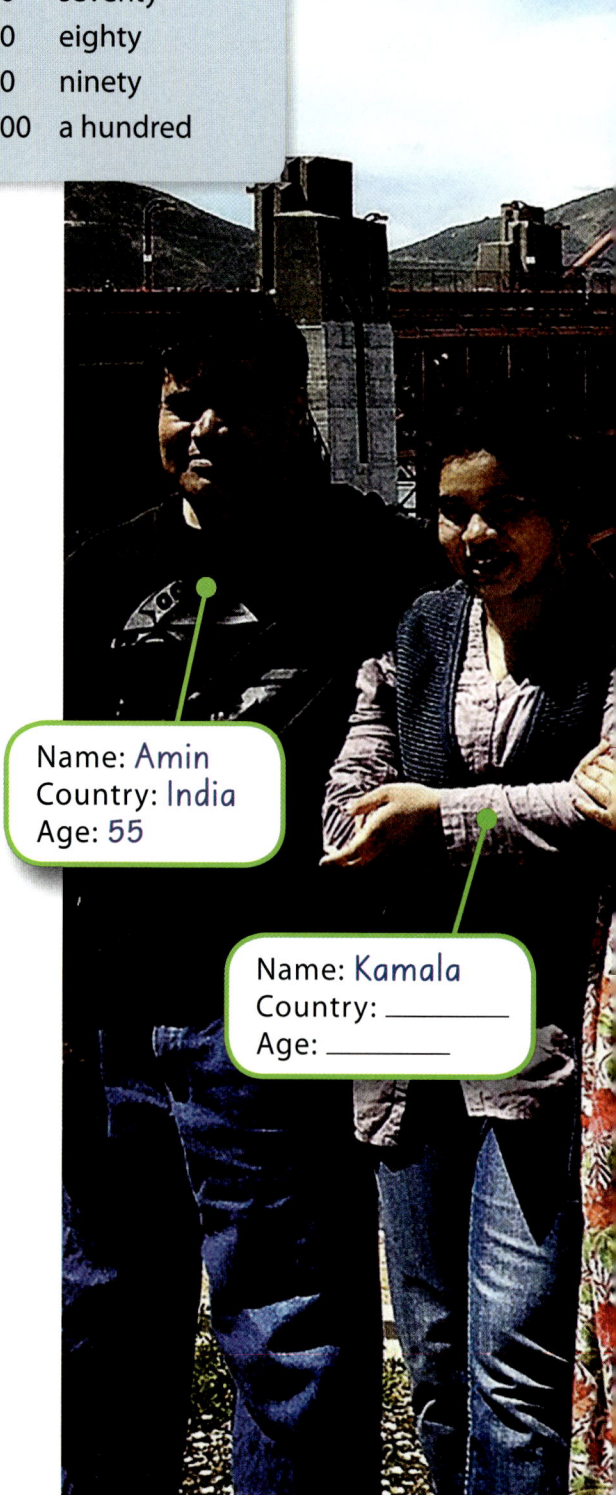

Name: Amin
Country: India
Age: 55

Name: Kamala
Country: _____
Age: _____

The place in the photo is in _____ .

a. Tokyo, Japan
b. Paris, France
c. San Francisco, the United States

Name: Katrin
Country: _____
Age: _____

Name: Sani
Country: India
Age: 49

Name: Angela
Country: _____
Age: _____

Ordinal Numbers 1st to 10th

| first | second | third | fourth | fifth | sixth | seventh | eighth | ninth | tenth | last |

A 🎧 17 **Listen and repeat.**

B **Work with a partner.** Take turns to guess the color bar.

Student A: Choose a color bar below.
Student B: Guess Student A's color bar.

1.
2.
3.
4.
5.
6.

What's the first color?

And the second?

It's green.

Listen. Complete the chart.

Name	Country	Colors	Position
Daniel Campbell	Trinidad and Tobago	white, red, _____	last
James Cooper	Australia	red, blue, _____	
Gavin Jones	the United Kingdom	red, white, _____	
Andres Rodríguez	Colombia	yellow, blue, _____	
Lucas Santos	Brazil	blue, green, ___yellow___	1st

D **Work with a partner.** Talk about the people in the race.

This person is in red, black, and white. He's last.

Where's he from?

He's from Trinidad and Tobago.

Months of the Year

A 🎧 19 **Listen and repeat.**

B **Talk with a partner.**

> **11th and 12th**
> 11th: eleventh
> 12th: twelfth

> What's the fourth month?

> It's April.

2013 2014 2015 2016 2017

January

M	T	W	T	F	S	S
						1
2	3	4	5	6	7	8
9	10	11	12	13	14	15
16	17	18	19	20	21	22
23	24	25	26	27	28	29
30	31					

February

M	T	W	T	F	S	S
		1	2	3	4	5
6	7	8	9	10	11	12
13	14	15	16	17	18	19
20	21	22	23	24	25	26
27	28					

March

M	T	W	T	F	S	S
		1	2	3	4	5
6	7	8	9	10	11	12
13	14	15	16	17	18	19
20	21	22	23	24	25	26
27	28	29	30	31		

April

M	T	W	T	F	S	S
					1	2
3	4	5	6	7	8	9
10	11	12	13	14	15	16
17	18	19	20	21	22	23
24	25	26	27	28	29	30

May

M	T	W	T	F	S	S
1	2	3	4	5	6	7
8	9	10	11	12	13	14
15	16	17	18	19	20	21
22	23	24	25	26	27	28
29	30	31				

June

M	T	W	T	F	S	S
			1	2	3	4
5	6	7	8	9	10	11
12	13	14	15	16	17	18
19	20	21	22	23	24	25
26	27	28	29	30		

July

M	T	W	T	F	S	S
					1	2
3	4	5	6	7	8	9
10	11	12	13	14	15	16
17	18	19	20	21	22	23
24	25	26	27	28	29	30
31						

August

M	T	W	T	F	S	S
1	2	3	4	5	6	
7	8	9	10	11	12	13
14	15	16	17	18	19	20
21	22	23	24	25	26	27
28	28	30	31			

September

M	T	W	T	F	S	S
			1	2	3	
4	5	6	7	8	9	10
11	12	13	14	15	16	17
18	19	20	21	22	23	24
25	26	27	28	29	30	

October

M	T	W	T	F	S	S
						1
2	3	4	5	6	7	8
9	10	11	12	13	14	15
16	17	18	19	20	21	22
23	24	25	26	27	28	29
30	31					

November

M	T	W	T	F	S	S
	1	2	3	4	5	
6	7	8	9	10	11	12
13	14	15	16	17	18	19
20	21	22	23	24	25	26
27	28	29	30			

December

M	T	W	T	F	S	S
				1	2	3
4	5	6	7	8	9	10
11	12	13	14	15	16	17
18	19	20	21	22	23	24
25	26	27	28	29	30	31

C **Work in a group.** Ask people in your group about their birthday.

> What month is your birthday?

> My birthday is in January.

The Real World

Seasons

Iguazu Falls,
Argentina,
in spring

 spring  summer  fall  winter

A 🎧 20 **Listen.** Complete the chart with the seasons.

Countries	March to May	June to August	September to November	December to February
South Korea	spring			winter
Argentina	fall		spring	

B **Work with a partner.** Look at the chart. Talk about the seasons in the two countries.

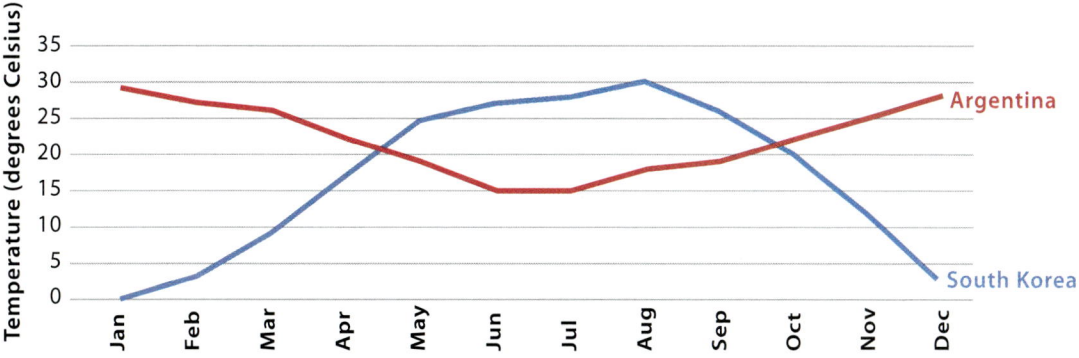

In December, it's winter in South Korea. It's three degrees.

Around the World

ABOUT THE VIDEO

Learn about different countries around the world.

aurora borealis over Lapland, Sweden

BEFORE YOU WATCH

Talk with a partner. Look at the countries in the box.
What continents are they in?

France	Japan	Australia	Canada
Brazil	Egypt	United Kingdom	Argentina

> France is in Europe.

WHILE YOU WATCH

A **Watch the video.** Write the order in which you see
the countries in the video.

_____   _____first_____   _____

_____   _____   _____

B **Watch the video again.** Complete the chart.

Country	China	Australia	South Africa	the United States	Sweden	Brazil
Continent		Australia	Africa			South America
Number of People	1.4 billion	23 million	____ million	318 million	____ million	____ million
Temperature	____ °C	____ °C	27°C	____ °C	0°C	30°C

AFTER YOU WATCH

Work with a partner. Put the countries in
size order—from big to small.

> First is China. There are 1.4 billion people in China.

BIG NUMBERS

1 thousand	=	1,000
1 million	=	1,000,000
1 billion	=	1,000,000,000

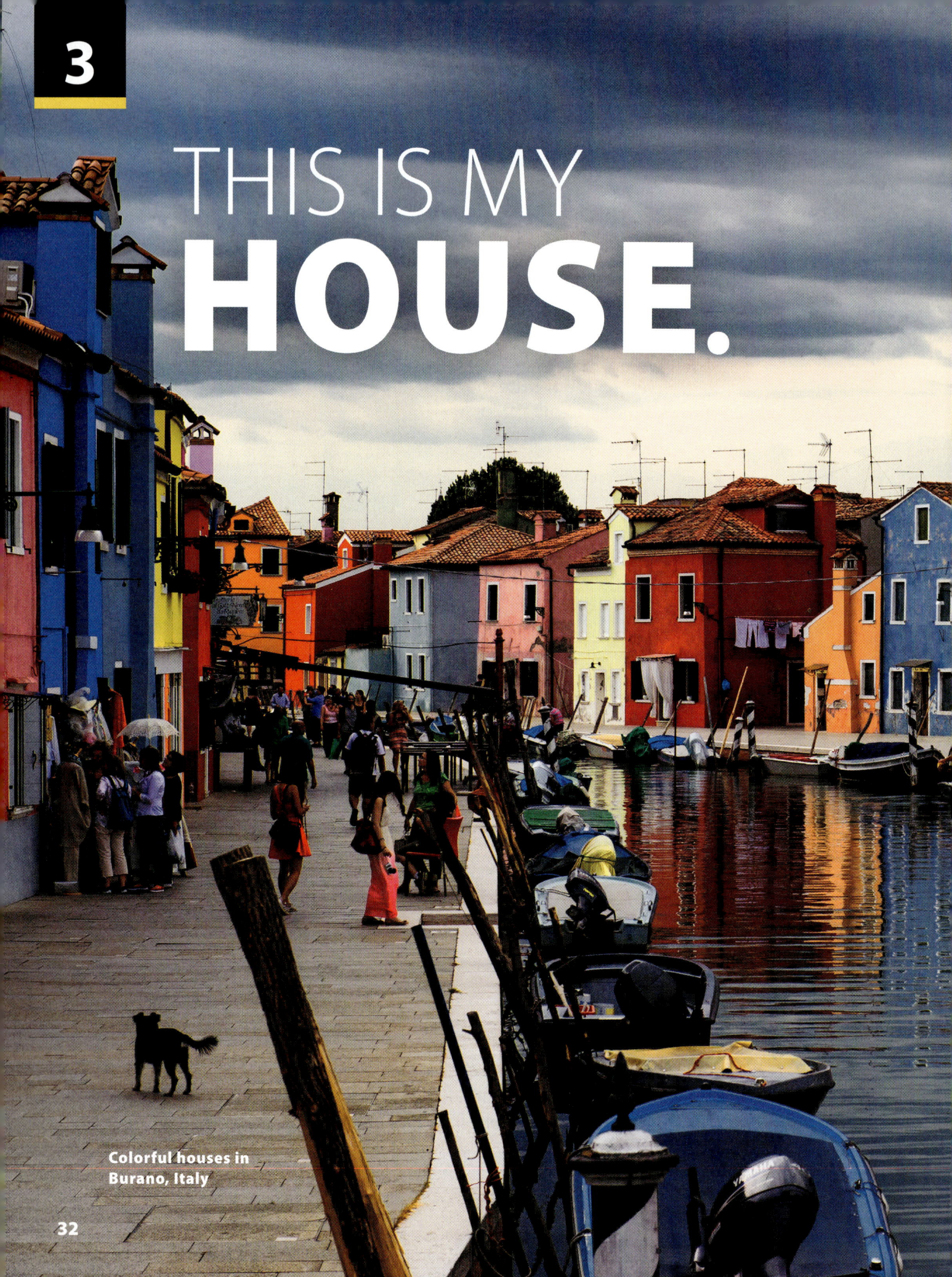

3

THIS IS MY
HOUSE.

**Colorful houses in
Burano, Italy**

Ordinal Numbers 11th to 31st

A 🎧 21 **Listen and complete.**

> fifteenth   thirty-first   twenty-sixth   twentieth
> nineteenth   thirtieth   twenty-third   ~~twelfth~~

11th	eleventh	18th	eighteenth	25th	twenty-fifth
12th	_twelfth_	19th	_____	26th	_____
13th	thirteenth	20th	_____	27th	twenty-seventh
14th	fourteenth	21st	twenty-first	28th	twenty-eighth
15th	_____	22nd	twenty-second	29th	twenty-ninth
16th	sixteenth	23rd	_____	30th	_____
17th	seventeenth	24th	twenty-fourth	31st	_____

May 1st
May Day

May 10th
Mothers' Day
in Mexico

May 5th
Children's Day
in Japan

May 28th
Hamburger Day
in the United
States

May

Monday	Tuesday	Wednesday	Thursday	Friday	Saturday	Sunday
1	2	3	4	5	6	7
8	9	10	11	12	13	14
15	16	17	18	19	20	21
22	23	24	25	26	27	28
29	30	31				

B **Look at the calendar.** Complete the sentences.

1. May Day is May ____1st____ .

2. Children's Day in _____ is May _____ .

3. Mothers' Day in _____ is _____ .

4. Hamburger Day in the United States is _____ .

C 🎧 22 **Listen.** Circle the numbers you hear.

1. (five)   fifth   5.   twenty   twentieth

2. eight   eighth   6.   twenty-four   twenty-fourth

3. ten   tenth   7.   twenty-nine   twenty-ninth

4. fifteen   fifteenth   8.   thirty   thirtieth

D 🎧 23 **Listen.** Circle the correct answers.

1. What (**day** / **date**) is it? It's September (**6th** / **16th**).

2. When is the (**first** / **last**) day of the holiday? It's March (**20th** / **23rd**).

3. When is the last day of (**spring** / **winter**)? It's (**March** / **May**) 30th.

4. When is (**her** / **your**) birthday? It's (**April** / **August**) 16th.

E **Talk with a partner.** Ask and answer questions about special days.

When is May Day?

It's May 1st.

When is your birthday?

It's July 23rd.

Children's Day in Japan

My Pets

A blue and yellow macaw

A 🎧 24 **Listen.** Write the animals you hear.

cat   dog   rabbit   fish   ~~bird~~   mouse

1. _____bird_____   2. _____   3. _____

4. _____   5. _____   6. _____

B Write the missing words.

1. a dog   two _____dogs_____

2. a bird   four _____

3. a cat   six _____

4. a rabbit   nine _____

> **IRREGULAR PLURALS**
>
> mouse **mice**   fish **fish**

C Circle the correct word.

SINGULAR	PLURAL
This is a cat.	**These** are cat**s**.
That is a rabbit.	**Those** are rabbit**s**.

1. (**This** / **These**) are dogs.   3. (**That** / **Those**) are his pets.

2. (**That** / **Those**) is my desk.   4. What's (**this** / **those**)?

D **Complete the conversation.** Look at the picture below.
Use the words in the box.

Pedro: What's the _____man's name_____?

Katy: His name is Robert.

Pedro: What's _____?

Katy: His pet is a _____.

Pedro: What _____ is it?

Katy: It's _____.

dog

~~man's name~~

black

Robert's pet

color

E **Work with a partner.** Talk about the other people in the picture.

What's the woman's name?

Her name is Janice.

Marie   Robert   Max   Janice   Jack

Scooby   Daisy   Bella   Sunny   Bluebell

Parts of the Body

A 🎧 25 **Listen and repeat.** Label the parts of the body on the photo.

ear	leg	hair	foot	mouth
eye	arm	hand	~~head~~	nose

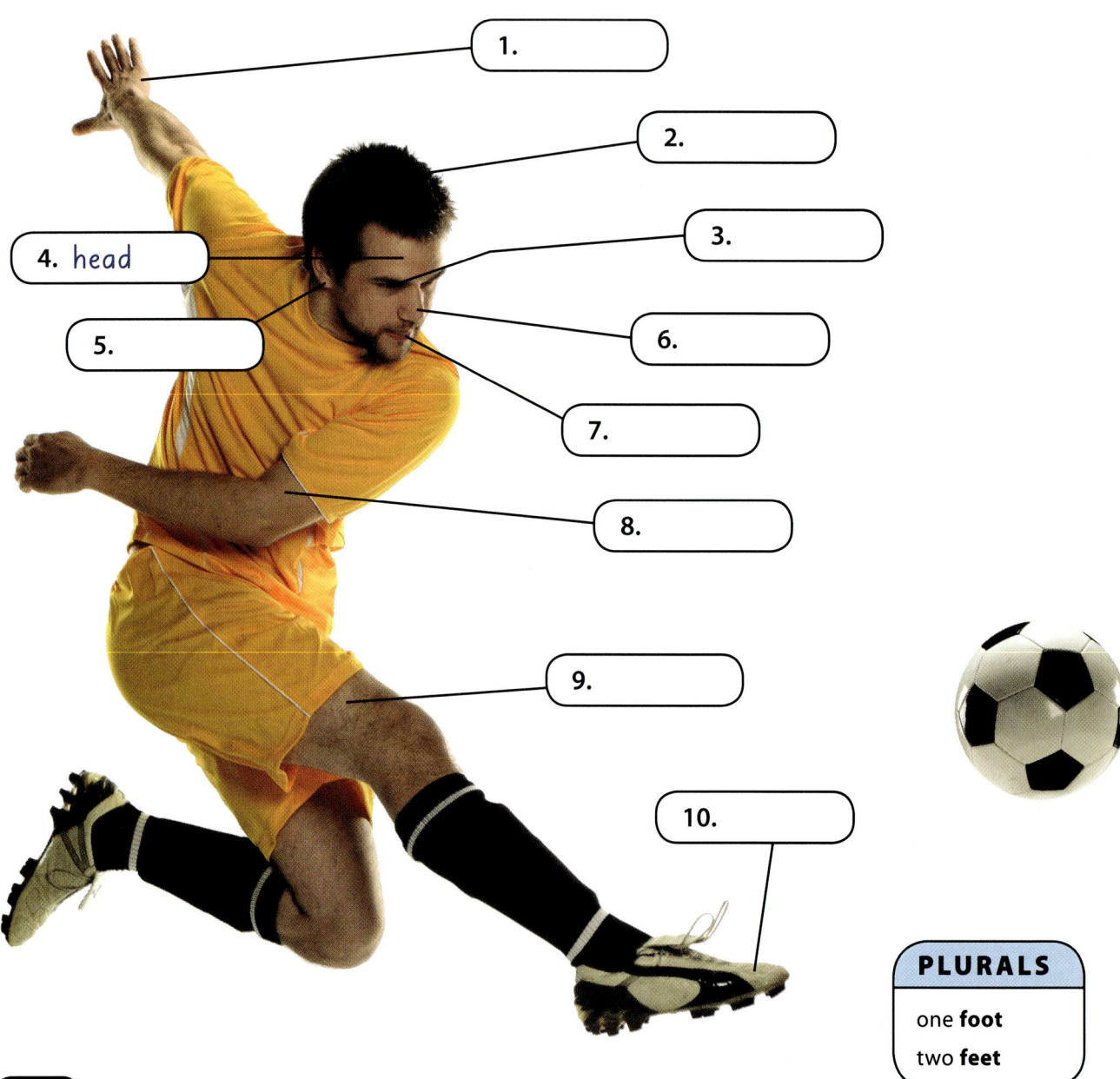

1.

2.

3.

4. head

5.

6.

7.

8.

9.

10.

PLURALS

one **foot**

two **feet**

B 🎧 26 **Listen.** Follow the instructions.

C **Work in a group.** Take turns to say instructions.

Touch your nose.

Touch your ear.

38 Unit 3

What Do You See?

Look at the body parts in the rock and on the building.

1.

2.

3. foot

A building in Thailand

A 🎧 27 **Listen.** Label the photos.

| ear | mouth | eye | ~~foot~~ | leg | nose |

B **Work with a partner.** Ask and answer questions about the photos with *this, that, these,* and *those.*

What's that?

That's the man's eye.

4.

5.

6.

A face in a rock in the United States

Around the House

A 🎧 28 **Look at the picture below.** Listen and repeat.

B 🎧 29 **Listen.** What part of the house is it?

1. ___bedroom___   2. _____   3. _____

4. _____   5. _____

C **Complete the questions and answers.** Replace the missing words to talk about other people in the house.

1. Where's _____Robert_____? ___He's___ in the _____.

2. What's ___his___ pet? It's a _____.

3. What color is _____ pet? It's _____.

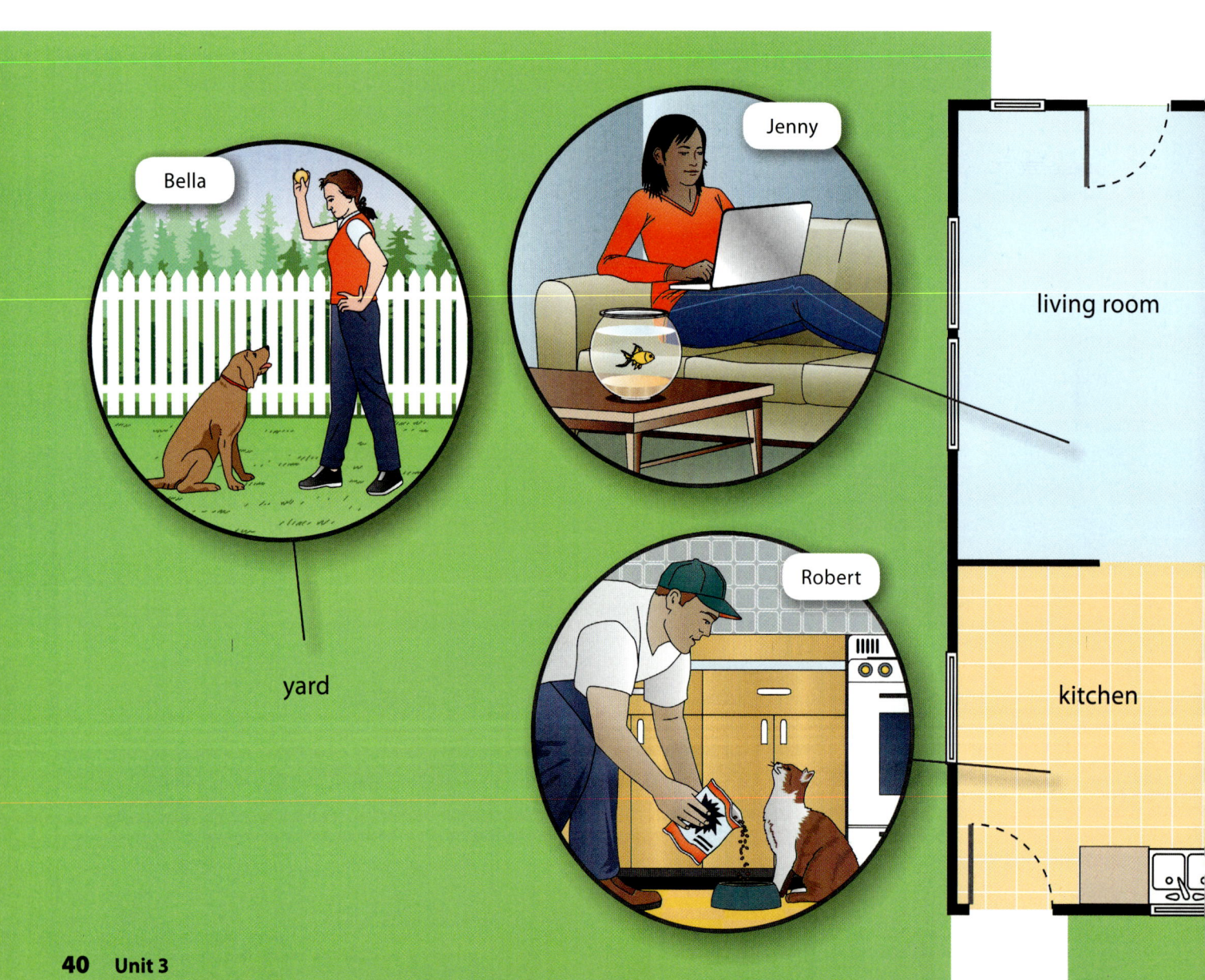

Bella

Jenny

Robert

yard

living room

kitchen

D **Talk with a partner.** Ask and answer questions about the picture.

What's her name?

Is the cat in the kitchen?

Her name is Bella.

Yes, it is.

Are the books in the living room?

No, they aren't.

E **Draw a floor plan of your house.** Talk with a partner about your house.

This is the kitchen. This is my bedroom.

bedroom

bedroom

bathroom

bedroom

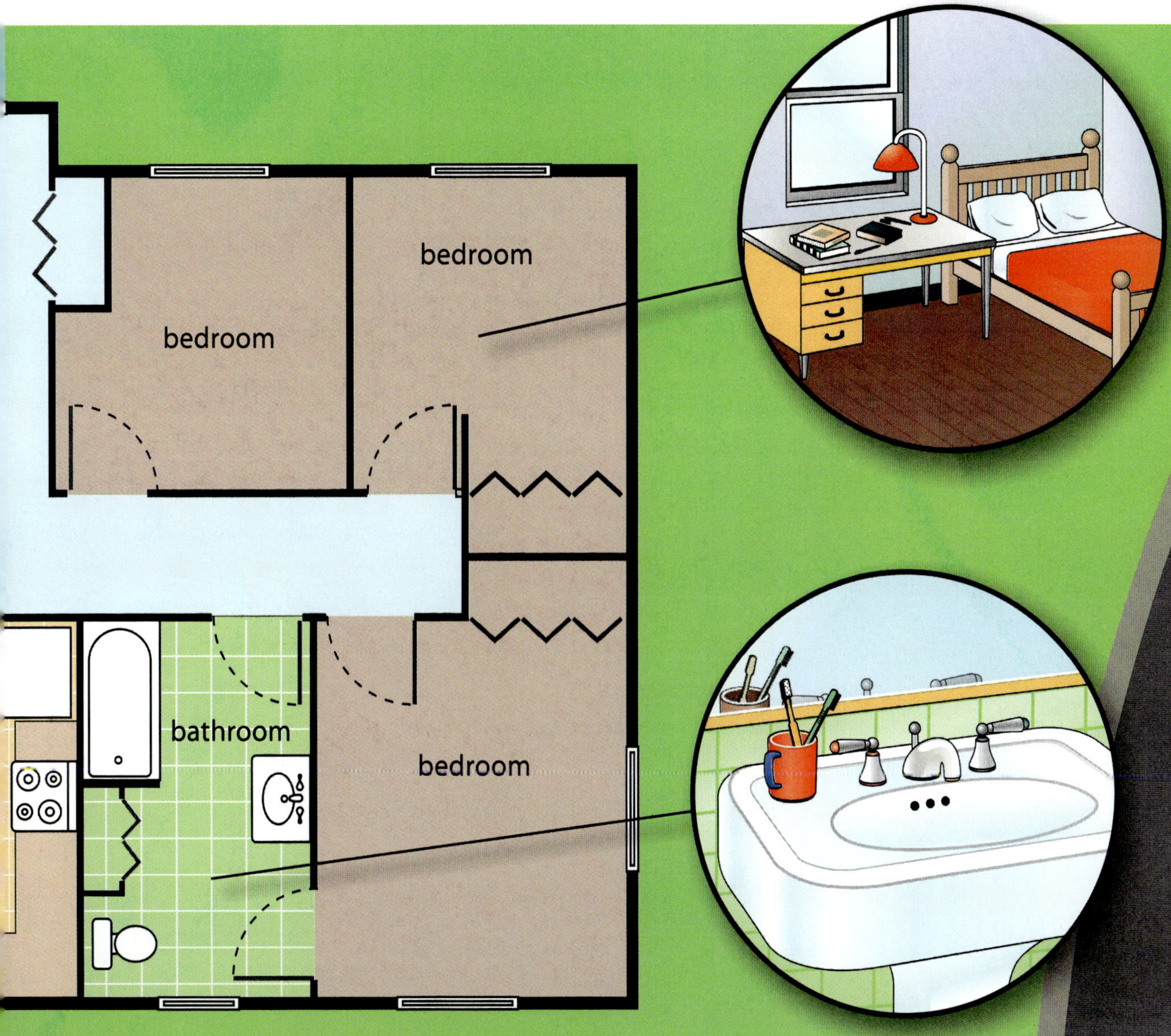

Otters in the House

1. eye

2.

3.

4.

5.

River otters in Alaska, United States

BEFORE YOU WATCH

Label the photo. Use the words in the box.

arm   ~~eye~~   mouth   nose   hair

WHILE YOU WATCH

A **Look at the photos.** Where are the otters?

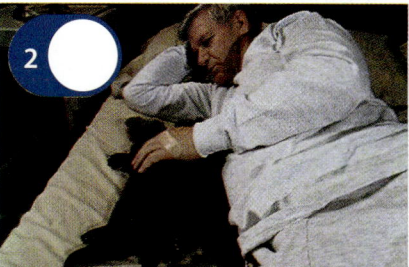

a. in the bathroom   c. in the kitchen

b. in the bedroom   d. in the yard

B **Watch the video.** Circle the correct answers.

1. The people are from (**the U.S.** / **Australia**).

2. Their pets are (**two** / **three**) otters.

3. The otters' names are (**Babyface and Little Paddles** / **Glen and Jeannie**).

4. The otters are (**brown** / **red**).

AFTER YOU WATCH

Talk with a partner. Answer the questions.

1. Do you want a pet otter?   2. What pet do you want?

What pet do you want?

I want a rabbit.

HELLO!

Vocabulary

A **Match.** Join the capital letters to the lowercase letters.

A ○	○ f	I ○	○ m	Q ○	○ t
B ○	○ e	J ○	○ k	R ○	○ q
D ○	○ a	K ○	○ i	S ○	○ y
E ○	○ g	L ○	○ j	T ○	○ r
F ○	○ b	M ○	○ l	U ○	○ s
G ○	○ h	N ○	○ p	Y ○	○ z
H ○	○ d	P ○	○ n	Z ○	○ u

B **Complete the words.** Use the chart.

one	two	three	four	five	six	seven	eight	nine	ten
a	o	e	b	s	k	p	d	n	r

1. <u>p</u> <u>e</u> <u>n</u>
   7 3 9

2. __ __ __ __ __ __
   3 10   5 3 10

3. __ __ __ __
   8 3   6

4. __ __ __ __
   4 2   6

5. __ __ __ __ __
   4 2 1 10

6. __ __ __ __ __
   7 1 7   10

C **Write the missing numbers.**

1. ten – eight = _____two_____

2. one + _____ = seven

3. three × three = _____

4. _____ × two = ten

5. seven – three = _____

6. four × two = _____

Grammar

A **Circle the correct answers.**

1. Hello (**Stig** / **stig**).　　2. It's a (**chair** / **Chair**).

3. My name is (**maya** / **Maya**).　4. It's (**Thursday** / **thursday**).

B **Complete the sentences.** Write *a* or *an*.

1. It's ___a___ board.　　2. It's _____ eraser.　　3. It's _____ blue pencil.

4. It's _____ orange pen.　5. It's _____ desk.　　6. It's _____ white computer.

C **Complete the conversation.** Use the words in the box.

> Hi　　What's your name　　~~I'm~~　　How do you spell your name

Kate:　Hello. _____I'm_____ Kate. _____?

Rob:　　_____, Kate. My name is Rob.

Kate:　_____?

Rob:　　R-O-B.

Kate:　Nice to meet you, Rob.

D **Complete the conversation.** Use the words in the box.

> that　　　English book　　　computer　　　~~this~~

1. Sam:　　What's _____this_____?

　Gabriela: It's an _____.

2. Gabriela: What's _____?

　Sam:　　It's my _____.

Vocabulary

A Unscramble the words.

1. aSuratdy   _Saturday_   5. nSudya   _____

2. ynaMdo   _____   6. naesdWdey   _____

3. draiyF   _____   7. ayhrsTud   _____

4. udseTya   _____

B Complete the crossword puzzle. Look at the clues in the photo.

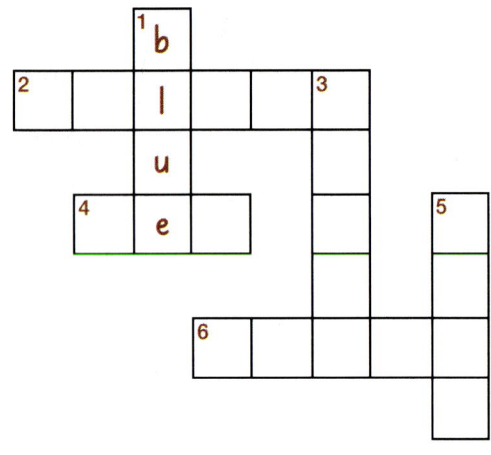

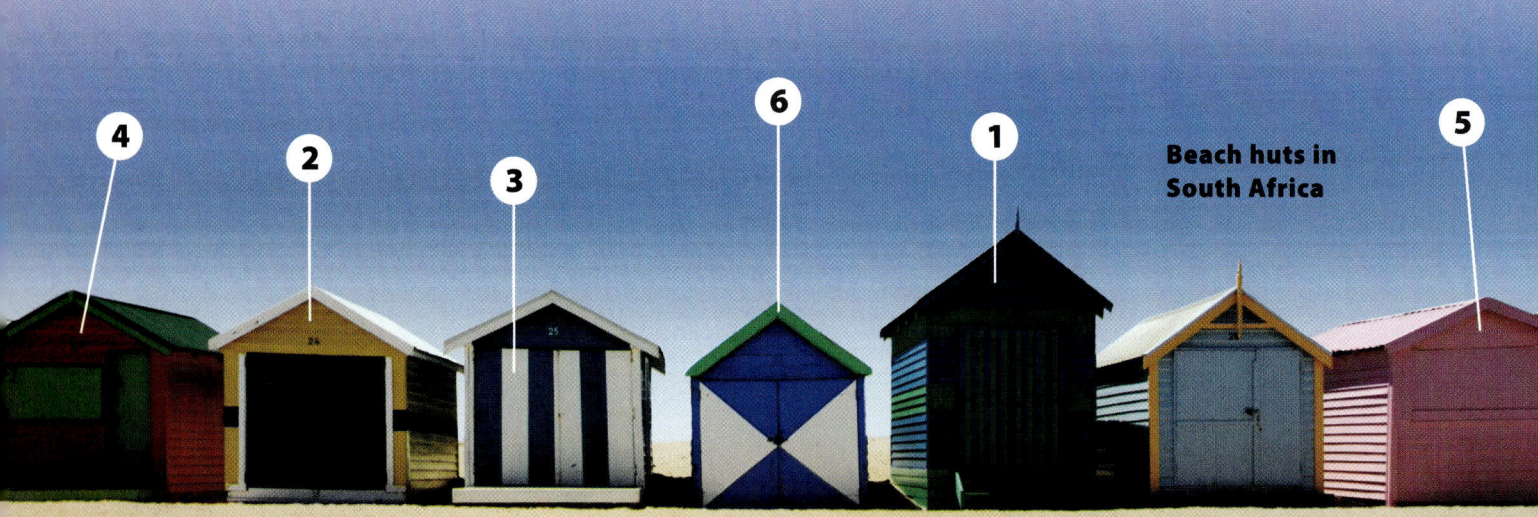

Beach huts in South Africa

Grammar

A **Rewrite the sentences.**

1. What is that? __What's that?__

2. It is a computer. _____

3. I am ten. _____

4. My name is Ryan. _____

5. She is Kelly. _____

B **Match.** Join the symbols to the classroom items.

1. ○   ○ a white eraser

2. ○   ○ a brown chair

3. ○   ○ a black computer

4. ○   ○ a red pen

5. ○   ○ a blue pencil

6. ○   ○ a yellow book

C **Circle the correct answers.**

1. Alan: (**What's** / (**What**)) color is the computer?

   Catalina: (**It** / **It's**) black.

2. Mika: What day is (**it** / **it's**)?

   Pete: It's (**yesterday** / **Saturday**).

3. Luis: What's (**that** / **day**)?

   Sarah: It's (**a** / **an**) English dictionary.

4. Jessica: (**Hi** / **Bye**)! What's your name?

   Daniel: My (**name** / **name's**) Daniel.

2

WHERE'S HE FROM?

Vocabulary

A **Complete the word search.** Find six different places.

A	N	T	A	R	C	T	I	C	A	A
O	S	W	E	D	E	N	E	D	O	S
L	A	U	S	T	R	A	L	I	A	I
P	N	A	T	Y	A	F	R	I	C	A
T	R	I	B	R	A	Z	I	L	E	D

Country	Continent
the United States	North America
	South America
China	
South Africa	
	Europe
	Australia
	Antarctica

B **Complete the chart.** Use the places in **A**.

C **Write the numbers.**

1. nineteen   twenty   twenty-one   <u>twenty-two</u>

2. twelve   fourteen   _____   eighteen

3. forty-two   thirty-nine   thirty-six   _____

4. ninety   eighty   seventy   _____

5. _____   forty-two   fifty-four   sixty-six

Grammar

A **Rearrange the words to make sentences.** Then match the questions to the answers.

1. your / What's / name

   ___What's your name___ ? ○

   a. I'm / Brazil / from

   ○ _____ .

2. How / are / old / you

   _____ ? ○

   b. in / It's / South America

   ○ _____ .

3. are / Where / you / from

   _____ ? ○

   c. name's / My / Gabriela

   ○ ___My name's Gabriela___ .

4. that / Where's

   _____ ? ○

   d. fourteen / I'm

   ○ _____ .

Name	Mike	Wendy	Anton
Country	South Africa	China	Sweden
Age	32	48	29

B **Complete the conversations.** Write questions or answers.

1. Lucy: ___Where's Mike from___ ?

   Daniel: He's from South Africa.

   Lucy: _____ ?

   Daniel: He's thirty-two.

2. Sofia: Where's Wendy from?

   Alan: _____ .

   Sofia: How old is she?

   Alan: She's _____ .

3. Hana: Where's Anton from?

   Jorge: _____ .

   Hana: _____ ?

   Jorge: _____ .

Vocabulary

A **Complete the chart.**

first	1st		6th
second	2nd	seventh	
third		eighth	
	4th		9th
fifth		tenth	

B **Rearrange the letters.** Write the months of the year.

1. ueJn   __June__   4. pSetbrmee   _____

2. cbOreto   _____   5. uJyl   _____

3. evbmeorN   _____   6. yMa   _____

C **Complete the puzzle to find the secret word.** Use the clues below.

1	s	u	m	m	e	r
2						
3						
4						
5						
6						

Clues:

1. It's hot in this season.

2. It's the first month of the year.

3. It's the third month of the year.

4. It's the tenth month of the year.

5. It's the ninth month of the year.

6. It's the last month of the year.

The secret word is _____!

Fall at Mersey River, Canada

A race in Rieti, Italy

Grammar

A **Look at the chart.** Circle **T** for True or **F** for False.

1. Iguider is first. **(T)** **F**
2. España is last. **T** **F**
3. Orth is from the U.S. **T** **F**
4. There are four people **T** **F**
   from Kenya.

B **Answer the questions.**

1. Who's second in the race?

   a. Lalang is second.

   b. Longosiwa is second.

2. Where's Merga from?

   a. He's from Ethiopia.

   b. He's from Kenya.

3. What position is Orth in the race?

   a. He's seventh.   b. He's ninth.

4. Where's Osako from?

   a. He's from Japan.   b. He's from Spain.

Position	Name		Country
1	Abdalaati IGUIDER		Morocco
2	Thomas Pkemei LONGOSIWA		Kenya
3	Lawi LALANG		Kenya
4	Ryan HILL		U.S.
5	Lopez LOMONG		U.S.
6	Suguru OSAKO		Japan
7	Imane MERGA		Ethiopia
8	Cornelius Kipruto KANGOGO		Kenya
9	Florian ORTH		Germany
10	Jesús ESPAÑA		Spain

THIS IS MY HOUSE.

Vocabulary

A **Label the photos.**

| rabbit | fish | ~~dog~~ | bird | cat |

1. _dog_   2. _____   3. _____   4. _____   5. _____

B **Complete the chart.**

eleventh	11th	twentieth		thirty-first		sixty-fifth	
twelfth		twenty-second	22nd	fifty-sixth		eighty-second	
seventeenth		twenty-eighth		forty-third		ninety-seventh	

C **Label the photo.**
Use the words in the box.

| ~~boy~~ | woman |
| man | girl |

1.

2.

3.

4. boy

Grammar

A **Circle the items in the picture.** Use the words in the box.

a desk	Maya's books	one orange chair	Stig's dictionary
a cat	Ming's pen	two yellow chairs	Nadine's computer

B **Circle the correct answers.**

Grace: What's (**this** / **those**)?

Tomas: It's Stig's dictionary.

Grace: What are (**that** / **these**)?

Tomas: They're Maya's books.

Grace: What are those?

Tomas: They're (**chairs** / **chair**).

C **Complete the conversation.**

Sara: What (**date** / **month**) is it today?

Danny: It's July 9th.

Sara: (**When** / **What**) is your birthday?

Danny: It's July 10th.

Sara: That's (**yesterday** / **tomorrow**)!

Danny: Yes, it is! When's your birthday?

Sara: It's April 1st.

Danny: Oh! That's April Fools' Day!

Vocabulary

A **Label the photo.**
Use the words in the box.

hand	leg
~~eye~~	foot
hair	nose
arm	

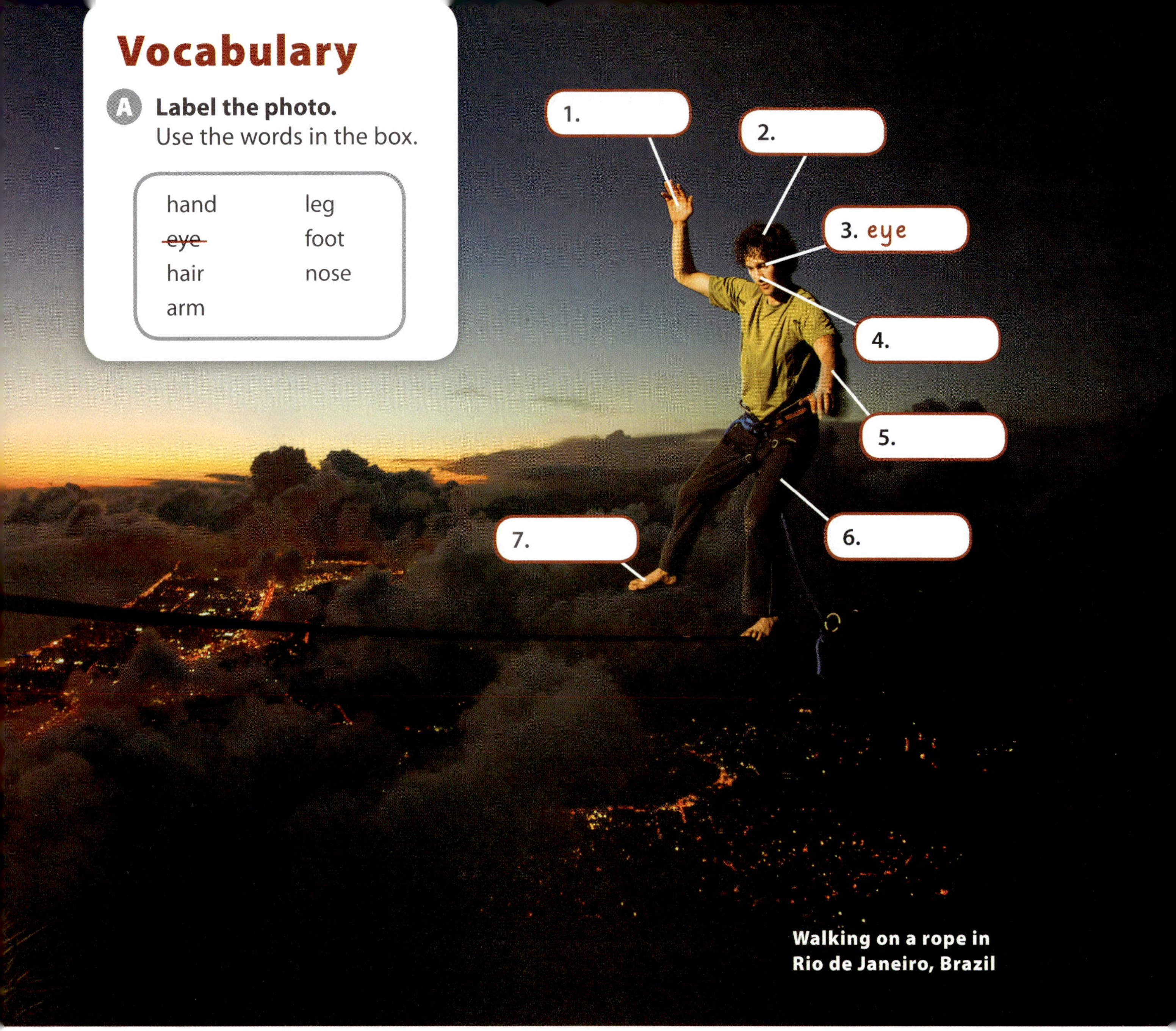

1.

2.

3. eye

4.

5.

6.

7.

Walking on a rope in Rio de Janeiro, Brazil

B **Look at the pictures.** Where do you find these things? Name the parts of the house.

1.  _____yard_____ 2.   _____ 3.  _____

4.   _____ 5. ▯ _____

Grammar

A **Write questions using the words in parentheses.** Then match the questions to the answers.

1. (TV / living room)

   <u>Is the TV in the living room?</u> ○   ○ a. No, they aren't.

2. (where / desk)

   <u>Where's the desk?</u> ○   ○ b. Yes, it is.

3. (chairs / bedroom)

   _____? ○   ○ c. They're in the bedroom.

4. (bed / kitchen)

   _____? ○   ○ d. It's in the living room.

5. (where / books)

   _____? ○   ○ e. No, it isn't.

B **Look at the photos.** Answer the questions.

1. Is the woman in the yard?

   <u>No, she isn't</u>.

2. Is the boy in the bedroom?

   _____.

3. Where are the cats?

   _____.

4. Is the dog in the house?

   _____.

5. Is the computer in the kitchen?

   _____.

REVIEW GAME

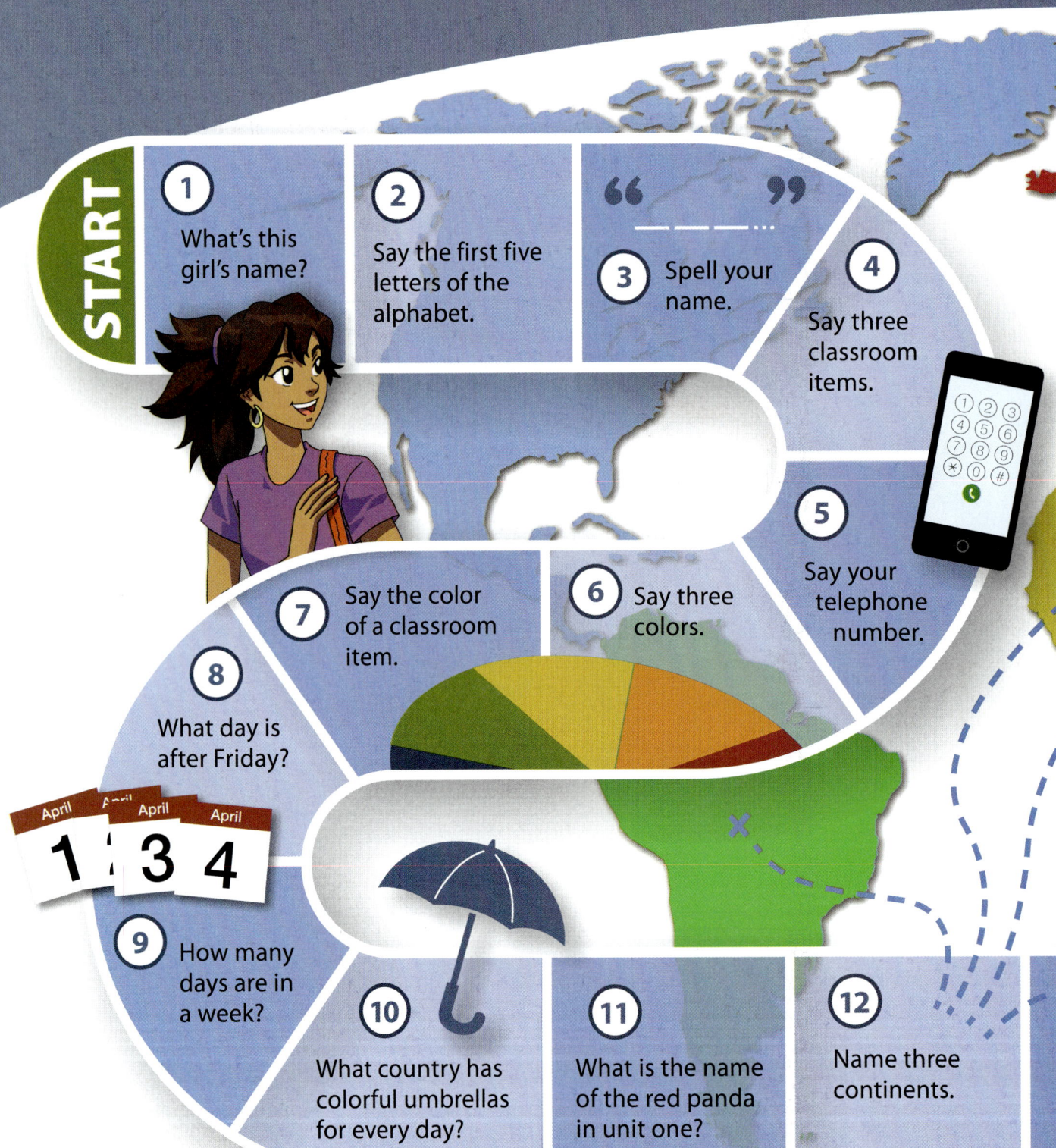

START

1. What's this girl's name?

2. Say the first five letters of the alphabet.

3. " _ _ _ _ ... " Spell your name.

4. Say three classroom items.

5. Say your telephone number.

6. Say three colors.

7. Say the color of a classroom item.

8. What day is after Friday?

9. How many days are in a week?

10. What country has colorful umbrellas for every day?

11. What is the name of the red panda in unit one?

12. Name three continents.

Play with 2–4 classmates. Take turns. Each classmate has a game counter.
Toss a coin and move your counter.

 **HEADS** Move **two** squares

 **TAILS** Move **one** square

 **?** Can't answer? **Miss a turn!**

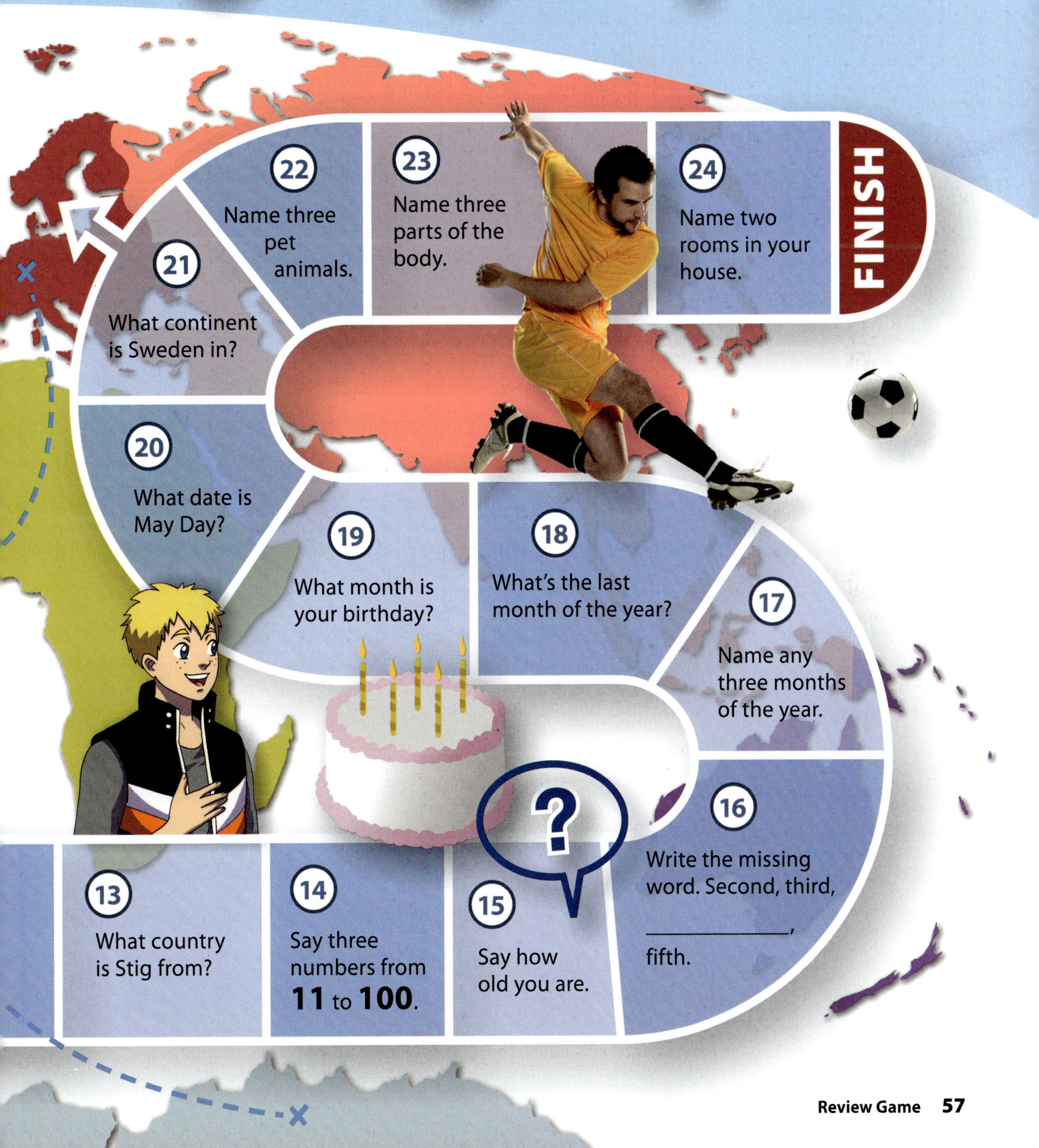

22 Name three pet animals.

23 Name three parts of the body.

24 Name two rooms in your house.

FINISH

21 What continent is Sweden in?

20 What date is May Day?

19 What month is your birthday?

18 What's the last month of the year?

17 Name any three months of the year.

16 Write the missing word. Second, third, _____, fifth.

?

13 What country is Stig from?

14 Say three numbers from **11** to **100**.

15 Say how old you are.

LANGUAGE NOTES

UNIT 1 HELLO!

Target Language

THE VERB *TO BE*

I'm	Nadine.
My name's	
It's	a pen.
It's	an eraser.
It's	purple.
That's	right.

WHAT QUESTIONS

What's				your name?
				this?
				that?
What	color	**is**	this?
What	day	**is**	it?

CLASSROOM INSTRUCTIONS

Stand up.
Listen.
Read.
Sit down.
Talk.
Write.
Open your book.
Close your book.
Look at the board.

HOW QUESTIONS WITH *DO*

How	do	you	spell	that?

Target Vocabulary

MEETING PEOPLE AND SAYING GOODBYE

Saying hello: Hello.; Hi.
Saying goodbye: Bye.
Saying your name: My name's Stig.; I'm Nadine.

CLASSROOM OBJECTS

pen, chair, paper, book, computer, eraser, board, desk, dictionary, pencil

NUMBERS

zero, one, two, three, four, five, six, seven, eight, nine, ten

COLORS

brown, red, yellow, pink, purple, white, blue, black, green, orange

DAYS OF THE WEEK

Monday, Tuesday, Wednesday, Thursday, Friday, Saturday, Sunday

UNIT 2 WHERE IS HE FROM?

Target Language

THE VERB *TO BE*		
I'm	from	Brazil.
It's	in	South Africa.
His name's	Tomas.	
He's	twenty-five.	
My birthday is	in November.	

WH- QUESTIONS (*WHAT* AND *WHERE*)—*HE/SHE/IT*		
What's	his	name?
Where's	she	from?

WH- QUESTIONS (*WHAT* AND *WHERE*)—*YOU*		
Where are	you	from?
What	month is	your birthday?

HOW QUESTIONS		
How old	is	he?
How old	are	you?

Target Vocabulary

CONTINENTS

Asia, Europe, Australia, North America, Africa, Antarctica, South America

COUNTRIES

Sweden, Brazil, South Africa, China, Macedonia, the United Kingdom, Romania, South Korea, France, Portugal, Spain, Trinidad and Tobago, Egypt, the United States, Argentina, Canada, India, Germany, Australia, Colombia, Japan

NUMBERS 11 TO 100

eleven, twelve, thirteen, fourteen, fifteen, sixteen, seventeen, eighteen, nineteen, twenty, twenty-one, thirty, forty, fifty, sixty, seventy, eighty, ninety, a hundred

ORDINAL NUMBERS (1ST TO 10TH)

first, second, third, fourth, fifth, sixth, seventh, eighth, ninth, tenth

MONTHS OF THE YEAR

January, February, March, April, May, June, July, August, September, October, November, December

SEASONS

spring, summer, fall, winter

LARGE NUMBERS

thousand, million, billion

UNIT 3 THIS IS MY HOUSE.

Target Language

DEMONSTRATIVES

This	**is**	a dog.
That		a fish.
These	**are**	mice.
Those		birds.

NOUN PLURALS

Singular (=1)	Plural (>1)
cat	cats
rabbit	rabbits
computer	computers

YES/NO QUESTIONS—HE/SHE/IT/THEY

Is	the cat	in the kitchen?	Yes, it is.
			No, it isn't.
Are	the books	in the living room?	Yes, they are.
			No, they aren't.

POSSESSIVE 'S

This	is	**Tom's**	bag.
Tom's	bag	is	blue.

WH- QUESTIONS (WHEN AND WHAT)—HE/SHE/IT

When is	your birthday?	My birthday **is**	April 8th.
What's	Jack's pet?	**It's**	a dog.
Where is	he?	**He's**	in the kitchen.
What	day is it?	**It's**	Saturday.

Target Vocabulary

ORDINAL NUMBERS 11TH TO 31ST

eleventh, twelfth, thirteenth, fourteenth, fifteenth, sixteenth, seventeenth, eighteenth, nineteenth, twentieth, twenty-first, twenty-second, twenty-third, twenty-fourth, twenty-fifth, twenty-sixth, twenty-seventh, twenty-eighth, twenty-ninth, thirtieth, thirty-first

PETS

cat, dog, rabbit, fish, bird, mouse

PARTS OF THE BODY

ear, leg, hair, foot, mouth, eye, arm, hand, head, nose

PLACES IN THE HOUSE

bedroom, bathroom, living room, kitchen, yard

Photo Credits

1 ones qiu/500px, **3** Tim Martin/Aurora Photos, **4–5** gary yim/Shutterstock, **8–9** Fred R. Conrad/The New York Times/Redux, **10** (b) Amy Toensing/NGC, **12–13** (t) Cengage Learning, **14–15, 58–59** Georgette Douwma/Getty Images, **16** (tl) Anna Kucherova/Shutterstock, (tc) Viktor Jarema/Shutterstock, **17** (t) Richard Nowitz/NGC, **18–19** Eddie Keogh/Reuters, **20–21, 60–61** Marko Djurica/Reuters, **24–25** Justin Sullivan/Getty Images, **26** (t) Cultura RM/Frank and Helena/Getty Images, **27** (b) Pete Saloutos/Image Source/Corbis, **29** gary yim/Shutterstock, **30–31** Babak Tafreshi/NGC, **31** (all) National Geographic, **32–33** Anan Charoenkal/Getty Images, **34** (bl) fotogestoeber/Shutterstock, (br) Viktor Jarema/Shutterstock, **35** AFP/Getty Images, **36** (t) lian_2011/Shutterstock, **38** Carlos E. Santa Maria/Shutterstock, **39** (t) Lars Hallström/age fotostock/Getty Images, (b) LeighSmithImages/Alamy, **41** (tr) Susan Biddle/White House/The LIFE Picture Collection/Getty Images, **42–43** Roy Toft/NGC, **43** (tl) (tr) (cl) (cr) National Geographic, **44** Joel Blit/Shutterstock, **46** Creativa Images/Shutterstock, **48** (t) StockbrokerXtra/Alamy, **49** (cl) Portra Images/Getty Images, (c) Blend Images/Shutterstock, (cr) Caiaimage/Chris Ryan/Getty Images, **50** (b) David Noton Photography/Alamy, **51** (t) Andreas Solaro/AFP/Getty Images, **52** (t) hadynyah/Getty Images, (cfl, **63**) Dorottya Mathe/Shutterstock, (cl) Maly Designer/Shutterstock, (c) Ferenc Szelepcsenyi/Shutterstock, (cr) Denis Tabler/Shutterstock, (cfr) aastock/Shutterstock, (b) Monkey Business Images/Shutterstock, **54** (t) Tim Kemple/NGC, **55** (cl) Chris Gramly/Getty Images, (cr) Image Source/Alamy, **57** (c) Carlos E. Santa Maria/Shutterstock

NGC = National Geographic Creative

Art Credits

7, 10, 12, 22, 23, 37, 45, 53, 56, 57 Raketshop, **17** (b) bioraven/Shutterstock, **22–23, 28, 29, 47, 56** Page2 LLC, **27** (t) Ints Vikmanis/Shutterstock, **36** bioraven/Shutterstock, **40–41** Scott MacNeill, **51** (b) xiver/Shutterstock, **54** (all symbols except tr) bioraven/Shutterstock, (tr) graphixmania/Shutterstock